I0224254

Abbreviate

For permissions and information on ordering books, contact operations@smallharborpublishing.com.

Cover art: Sarah Jarrett, "Levitation"
Cover design: Brianna Protesto
Editor: Joshua Davis
Publisher: Allison Blevins
Director: Kristiane Weeks-Rogers

ABBREVIATE
SARAH FAWN MONTGOMERY
ISBN 978-1-957248-50-9
Harbor Editions,
an imprint of Small Harbor Publishing

Abbreviate

Sarah Fawn Montgomery

Harbor Editions
Small Harbor Publishing

For the smallest versions of ourselves so that we might grow.

Contents

Abbreviate

Stomp

We blast off to nowhere, launching as far as we can get from the dust and tumbleweeds, the old railroad rattling though our town in search of somewhere safer, before gravity takes control and we come crashing down.

My aunt makes her living selling escape. She paints on her smile and shows her teeth as if the men can hear it over the phone. She purrs about airplanes and rocket ships, rail engines and submarines. Modeling is her trade, a world sold in miniature to anyone looking to pretend themselves plastic, wishing, like my aunt on her endless diets, they could shrink smaller.

She can sell almost anything, like a tiny motorboat, even though our town is so dry the river between my house and hers is all dried up, just a crack down the center where gaunt cats chase after baby rabbits who don't know enough yet to simply give up, their innards left on our porches as if to say love requires surrender. She can sell toy army soldiers like they're collectibles, even though her soldier husband was a safe choice like broccoli at dinner or coloring in the lines. He has a steady income from Vietnam and reminds her that Desert Storm is a real desert when she sleeps away long afternoons in her tiny pool, the plastic sides melting in the heat, her great breasts bobbing like buoys desperate to escape.

Once, she sold a toy car to a car salesman, instructing me to watch how to convince a man you have something he wants in order to get what you need. She made her commission before denying his, and then she took me to a movie where a bride escapes just before the big day, putting on her veil before lacing up her shoes to run.

My aunt's cluttered house is full of possibilities— a sprawling Victorian dollhouse, a submarine, a NASA replica, army tanks her husband says aren't as good as the ones he rode in during the war. She spends her life following directions, gluing parts together, painting over the seams. She knows that you make one mistake and the whole thing crumbles.

On weekends we wander into the dusty fields surrounding our town. They're full of yellow mustard dotting the land acidic, snake holes where rattlers seek the cool underground to rest coiled, ready to strike. The railroad slashing through town screams into the sky, and smoke like sulphur streams out of houses with the shades drawn.

We make our ways to the center of the field, through shotgun shells and syringes, deep where no one can find us if we shout, where the danger shimmers like the heat. My aunt's perfume makes something beautiful here but also makes it hard to breathe. She sets up the rocket launch, pointing it straight to the sky.

Her husband is away this weekend at an army base—control burning the land, setting fire to the golden hillsides—which is why she is lonely but also why her smile is real. It's why my smile is too, because I don't like how he hugs me too long, waves his hands in my face when I don't laugh at his jokes without punchlines, miscorrects my aunt and me with a loud voice like we can't understand unless he talks real slow. He has a uniform like the model soldiers we paint with tiny brushes, newspapers spread out to catch our mistakes, but his is dull, no stripes or patches, dirty green like the old truck he is always fixing, splayed underneath like a dead body.

Out here, my aunt uncoils. She makes her body as big as she can, strong enough to ignite. I don't like rockets like I don't like my uncle's spicy breath, the way his teenage son holds me down after he gets kicked out of the military, calls touching *tickling* and makes me feel like I want to run away.

My aunt insists I learn to explode. She instructs me to jump as high as I can, then fall hard. She shows me how far a rocket can escape if I stomp, use my whole body to send it soaring. Over and over we jump, ricocheting our weight onto the pump, the force of our determination shooting the rockets sharp as a slap. Sometimes they get so far away we can't see them at all, and we crane our heads at our power, breathless at the chance to witness a getaway.

All scorching summer we launch, sweat clinging to her heavy breasts and my growing ones, between our thighs where we bleed in secret. The heat is relentless, but so are we. Up and up they go, our eyes trained to the skies, the blazing hills and my uncle and the soldiers like him creeping slower, playing with fire.

Sometimes we lose a rocket in the tumbleweeds, scratch ourselves bloody trying to discover where it went, wondering how we could have lost sight.

Soon my uncle will be gone too, locked far enough away that we can finally breathe. The newspapers underneath our models and paint say that he ran over his ex-wife during a fight, crushed her body with his camouflage truck like a tank before coming home to correct and cuddle my aunt in the dark.

My aunt doesn't say much after he's locked away, simply smiles with her teeth to sell a story where she is fine, but she moves across the country, escapes before the fire is out.

After she's gone, I will remember the way it felt in her house, surrounded by frozen replicas, how we jumped to nowhere, using every part of ourselves in that lonely field to launch away and come crashing down. How all around us was dead. How we had to tiptoe to escape the snakes.

Planetarium

Overhead are stories big as the sky. The Big Dipper is a cup to lift to your lips like the beers the men in my family drink between cigarettes or the Diet Cokes the women sip all day, a little sweetness between their pinched shut lips. The stars make a big bear and a small bear, a big dog and a small dog, myth a way of teaching us how the world works. There is even a belt like the one my parents use to spank me if I am naughty, if I do not do my chores with a smile, if I talk back, if I complain too much about P.E. or how the boys at school chase me around during recess like we are playing tag, except I never said I wanted to be part of their game.

On elementary school field trips, I crouch as small as I feel along with the other girls to climb inside the dark dome. We sit under a pretend sky and listen to stories about the zodiac and Hercules. The boys throw spitballs or announce they are bored or try to correct the tour guide like they have seen their fathers do to their mothers. Later, when I try to explain the star stories I have learned in school to the men in my family, they will interrupt to explain what I am already telling them.

The planetarium guide asks us to tell the story of a woman who was so important that history placed her among the stars. She is hard to find, there in the darkness alongside Orion's belt and the centaur's arrow, even men's objects important enough to be immortalized. We search the heavens for a woman good enough to be remembered, but most women we know are remembered for misbehaving—the classmates who get expelled for kissing or crying, the teacher who got in trouble for wearing too much makeup, even hungry Eve falling for the trick where someone tells you not to do something and you are foolish enough to do anyway. Already, we know better than to try and play soccer when the boys say no girls allowed or to join a game of truth or dare where the only outcome is kissing some toady boy who teases us in history class and says we couldn't possibly know anything about war.

We spy Cassiopeia, a woman so vain as to know her own worth, to boast of her own beauty and that of her daughter to a God who would not accept this arrogance. She was banished to the heavens and forever chained to a throne of punishment. We spy her daughter, Andromeda, whose only wrongdoing was that her mother believed her beautiful, yet still she was chained to a rock at the edge of the sea for a monster to devour, only to be saved by a man who demanded she marry him in return for his heroism.

When we cannot find a woman who has not been banished to the darkness for some wicked doing, we imagine them. We see a woman with a skirt made of stars stretched wide across the sky like the broad hips of the women we come from. We see a woman who ran away from the earth to fling herself into the heavens so she could finally have some quiet. We see a girl with a dozen comebacks for playground taunts scattered like a galaxy. We see stars like soccer balls soaring cleanly into a goal.

The prizes, our guide adds, for answering correctly, are star-shaped erasers, mechanical pencils, lollipops filled with bubblegum that will turn your tongue blue as a universe. Over and over, the boys send their hands soaring like rockets into the sky. They wave them in front of our faces. They call out answers unprompted. They are wrong. Wrong again. They are wrong so many times that eventually the guide reveals the answers and rewards the boys just for trying.

We girls had the answers locked tightly inside. Sometimes they even slipped out, whispered under our breath or spoken aloud to see if anyone was listening or would believe we were capable of this knowledge.

On the bus home, the boys leave eraser burns on

our arms that will scab and scar. They poke us with pencils, and the teachers scold us when we scream. They blow bubbles in our faces just to watch them burst. Over and over, they tell the stories of their glories, how they were rewarded with prizes for their greatness. Back at school, everyone shares their tales in the halls like legends.

I curl invisible in my bus seat to avoid their attention. But I want to be someone seen. I want to be someone believed.

At dinner that night, I tell my parents I knew the answer, but nobody would call on me, and how the boys tried to steal attention even from stars. They tell me not to exaggerate, not to be so sensitive. They tell me to speak up, to try harder. When I get frustrated and cry, they tell me I am being a bad girl and send me to bed.

Under the covers, I look out the windows at the darkening sky. No one ignores the Milky Way. No one tells the moon what to do. I imagine myself as big as the heavens. I pretend I am so big my stories take up the sky.

Pocketed

Polly is as small as your fingernail but shiny and clean, not like your ragged half-moons, the ones you use to dig in the sandbox as though you are trying to escape, to drag across your thighs, leaving pale tracks, skin turned to dust as if to confirm how easily you can be reduced to nothing.

Polly wears a red headband around her blonde curls, and you try in the bathroom mirror, balancing on the sink, to see yourself as if for the first time, gangly gap-toothed girl playing dress-up behind the toothpaste spray. When you lean forward to magnify your desperation, you smell old food and the sharp sting of Listerine.

Polly keeps a dog and a cat at her country cottage, a basket of kittens and a koi pond at her parade village. She looks after animals in her veterinary hospital. They smile even though you know this isn't possible. Dogs like yours jump the metal fence to run away, choke themselves hoarse trying to escape the chain. Your haunchy cat slinks the yard like a premonition.

You find disemboweled mice on the porch—blue and yellow gut sacks, heads held on by strings. You feel that way sometimes, like you would drift away if not for the tether of your spine. Severed hands and feet—tiny as your plastic Polly Pocket, a dollhouse that fits in your palm—try to scurry off the cement.

The cat loves Mama best, brings her baby bunnies, wild-eyed and frozen. Mama pries them from the cat's jaws, walks into the field across the street—dead with weed and dust, broken bottles and cigarette butts— to set them free.

Polly hosts sleepovers in her pastel living room, volleyball parties on her private beach. Polly has a secret garden, a magic jungle.

No one comes to your sleepovers because last week a bar fight left a man dead on Main Street. Because the house by the riverbed pulses meth smoke like rotten eggs. Because the rusted-out cars look like piles of bones. Because your parents' fights about money are so big and loud that you hide beneath your bed. Because you said out loud that your swollen eyes make your lashes look like spiders when you look to the sky.

Make a fake beach in your sandbox, pretend stranded and please help. Struggle for air like drowning so good that sometimes you for real can't breathe. Make a garden of dirt clods. Hang ribbon from the doorway of your playhouse, pretend Polly walking through jungle vines. Pretend so good you imagine them snakes like in your nightmares, all that thrash and gnash in the sheets trying to escape.

Polly's houses are plastic compacts shaped like a star, like a flower, soapsuds, a seashell. Polly fits inside anything beautiful. Polly makes any place a home. She even fits in your hand-me-down pocket, the one sagging at the corner where you bury your hand, your head. Where you try to climb inside.

Your house is getting bigger, like the unhappiness is pushing out the walls. Or maybe it's you getting smaller. Your clothes don't fit right, your bed's too wide. You must be imagining it, you think, even the thought too big for your skull, floating out and above your head. Your plastic bank, the empty girl you drop pennies into, is nearly your height now, and even the ballerina in your music box twirls large in front of your face.

Your feelings don't fit, like how a feel slips out of your mouth and you say *stop* or *no*, your heart struggling inside your smallness, aorta pumping at your throat.

Polly's smile has worn off under your frantic fingers, but you draw one in red pen to match your own wavering line.

There are rattlesnakes in the yard, black widows in the eves, sex predators down the street.

Your neighbor spies from his window, whispers through the knothole in the fence that he watches you undress. Your other neighbor never sleeps, mutters on the porch about ghosts, pops his head over the fence when you take out the garbage to say it's the end of the world.

You crouch when you undress, try to hide from the man peering inside your pastel room. You hold plastic still.

You crouch smaller when you take out the garbage, bones splitting the bag, revealing the gnaw where someone sucked out the sweet marrow. Alcohol bottles bang your shins, leave them purple like the circles under your parents' tired eyes.

You crouch smallest to escape the neighbor's arms reaching over the fence toward you, pleading, "Let me save you, girl."

Daddy watches boxing on TV while you play Polly in her tiny jewel house. You listen to the sound of fists on flesh and shrink. Now you fit in the suitcase Mama is rolling to the front door, the hole she punched in the wall, the one Daddy kicked too.

Polly grows and grows, or you shrink and shrink, and now she is bigger than your nail, your finger, your whole clenched hand, tendons tight against the cage of your skin.

One man punches another, teeth down the throat. Blood spatters across the screen like stars, the twinkle lights in Polly's enchanted garden.

You climb inside Polly's house when Mama closes the door. The tiny dog and cat meet you. The koi fish leap from the pond in greeting. You smell the sterile safe of plastic. You walk the path, sit quiet on the bench. Everywhere is green. There are no neighbors. You can't even find Polly.

Inside the house, the bed is big enough for one. The couch too. There is no fighting on TV. There is no toothpaste on the bathroom mirror when you check your Polly hair, Polly smile.

Grab the lid, snap the compact closed. Now you are hidden, safe in this brittle plastic heart.

Giving Up

Rainy days, we practice giving up.

We fill the middle school locker room with cheap vanilla body spray that vanishes like the candy necklaces we loop like nooses around our necks. We open lockers too small to store the backpacks that shrink us closer to the ground. Even our wet footprints are eager to disappear.

The rain makes our clothes stick to our bodies— we are slick with the reminder that we exist to be hidden. Teachers throw sweatshirts at girls in white shirts the same way they send us home when our fingers don't reach past our shorts or a bra shows when we bend to tie our shoes. We've given up on wearing sandals and tank tops like the boys, the Lost & Found mostly our confiscated clothes hanging from the rack like ghosts.

Girl bodies are to be covered, which is why we have to wear PE clothes approved by the PTA, dispensed a size or two too big, shrouding our bodies like a secret, like shame.

It's no secret Brittany has the biggest boobs, enough to fill bra cups while the rest of us struggle to fill the training bras that make our fathers flinch. She shows us her bra the way she shows the boys her breasts for the thrill and a little money. The cups and hooks and straps are pieces of a puzzle we are trying to put together, like how to shave our legs without stripping slivers of skin or how to suck in our stomachs so our ribs show like frightened wings to help us escape.

When it rains, we give up the chance to go outside at all. We watch the boys from behind the opaque windows of our locker room. They race to see who can slide the farthest on the wet blacktop. They jump in every puddle to see how much water they can displace. They look up to the sky, opening their mouths to savor the taste.

Inside we look up at the skylight, rain pounding hard on the glass overhead. It is crowded, bodies crammed into the tiny rows of lockers. They are small enough our backpacks don't fit but our bodies do on a dare. Dawn fits, and Tori, who is so small she still wears children's clothes and eventually gets a bone disease for old people. We crowd around while they beg us to close the door like a coffin.

All spring we exercise inside, testing our bodies like how the teacher pinches the fat on our arms and legs and calls out the measurements for the class to hear. She counts how far we can bend in half to reach forward for an invisible prize, and counts our vertebrae to see if we are growing straight, sighing at the girls whose spines aren't clear lines for her to see.

When we run out of tests to fail, we line up single file down the rows of lockers, trying to call to each other over the tops, though our voices vanish overhead like specters. We know what to expect from a tiny TV in front of us, just like we know that girls can only hit softballs and aren't allowed to play hockey, just like soon we will have to learn to square dance with the boys who stomp on our feet and complain like we're the ones who picked the stupid activity when we'd rather play field hockey or dance choreo like on MTV.

The man on TV has a curl halo and a red tank top, and his fingers go way past his tiny shorts. He waves his arms, stepping to the beat of a song only the teacher knows.

"Faster, ladies," he shouts, sidestepping, and when we can't keep up because there is no room, our gym teacher says, "Get smaller," meaning shrink yourself to fit. We take tiny steps, trying to move in rhythm without moving at all. We break a sweat, tired from the effort of erasure.

We get small like how Tasha hasn't eaten in a month because she didn't fit in a locker, throwing up now before class, or how Becky can't sit cross-legged for attendance without bruising her tailbone. We get small like how we disappear in math class, all the problems about billiards and trains, imaginary men named Dave, and in history, too, the textbooks absent of women, though our teacher, a real man named Dave, reminds us we're special by picking us up at recess, spinning us around like we're dancing.

We wave our hands over our heads like frantic birds, hollow bones flying nowhere. We twist but don't shout, silent as important for girls as small, the teacher says after a few days trapped with us giggling inside. We squat and lunge until it burns.

"Push until your body gives up," our teacher reminds us.

Soon we're giving up crusts of sandwiches, pizza grease we blot with a napkin, our lunches altogether. We give up on saying the boys spit down our backs and grab our butts like we give up on saying the bus driver talks about our stomachs or that when we have a bad day the principal makes us hug him too close and too long and whispers in our ears that he'll never give up on us because he thinks we're more like a friend than a student.

The rain hits the glass ceiling hard, the windows fogged up with our collective vanishing. In front of us, the man on TV commands the women behind him. He reminds us that disappearance is a reward, erasure a pleasure.

Outside the boys run laps in the rain, competing to see whose stride is biggest before heading into the gym to spread out and lift weights, binge on carbs and protein shakes to get bigger.

We hear them laughing when the tape is over, before we rewind it to begin giving up all over again.

Light as a Feather, Stiff as a Board

The trick to feeling alive is to pretend you're already dead. Everyone knows this, but no one says.

Pizza is for ranch like Leo is for Kate, even though you mostly like him because his long hair makes him look like a girl kissing a girl, but the real kind, not Brittany kissing Marie to make the boys watch.

Dr. Pepper tastes like the Lip Smackers you slather around your mouth after gym class, slick like Crayola, red like a wound. When you swallow soda, you are drinking your own kiss, your own *sorry*, your own *help*.

Jelly bracelets are out and candy necklaces are in, a chalk-flavored noose around your neck, except tonight is for glow bracelets, the ones you crack like a body, like a secret, like a *love me* to light fluorescent under the false starry sky plastered on the ceiling of whoever is hosting the sleepover.

Orion is for losers, like science, like band, but everyone knows the Big Dipper is an empty bowl like your stomach exhaled when you dance, when you pose for pictures, when you play "Spice Up Your Life," even your favorite songs about food no one eats.

Dancing is for the dark, girl bodies a thing best shrouded, so off go the lights except for strings of purple flashes, the strobe making everyone ghoulish and disjointed. Exist between beat and breath. Feel a disappearance of your own making. Bump and grind like MTV, except with hipbones, tailbones, knobby knees. Sometimes someone gets an elbow to the face, a braces-bloody reminder that girl bodies are a liability, metal cage mouth a warning, a protection.

When the caffeine and sugar are sickly in your veins, smeared crystalline across your best impression of a smile, circle up to spill your guts. Who do you like, what about yourself do you hate, what is the truth you will dare to admit? Someone kissed a boy, someone called a sex line, someone gained five pounds, someone leaves to throw up in the bathroom again.

We form a circle around our hunger, another empty bowl. We are full of want and longing, the swell of desperation. We fool ourselves into thinking this is magic.

Light as a feather, stiff as a board, we chant, another command in unison. As always, we reach for the smallest girl, longing to hold her, though we are only permitted tentative fingertips. The trick to power is to pretend you don't want any.

This one has tiny bruises along her spine where the wooden floor proved too much. That one knocks soda on her pizza every time. This one will learn to smoke and forget how to aim the flame, singeing her smile.

You are praised for disappearing. For the way your stomach collapses on itself, simply giving up, or the way your ribs create a bowl around your hollowness. Sometimes you hide pennies in your clavicle, stones in the hollows at the small of your back to constellate, storytell your empty.

Earlier, in the hot tub, everyone sighed over the way your hipbones held out your bathing suit like a siren. They touched your hips, your stomach, hands sticky with heat and chlorine, with shimmer body spray leaving you smeared and glittering with their want. But no one wants you, just your not-a-body. You are only something because you are nothing.

Your sister has a doll that exists to eat. Her mouth moves by motor to chew plastic food that falls through a tube to her backpack. Take it out to feed her again, an endless cycle. Sometimes you put a finger between her rubbery lips to feel her pull at your heart, take you in. The hurt feels good. You like to tease her hunger, but really you are mocking yourself.

Hold fingers to one another's mouths to add glitter lip-gloss, to taste whipped body butter before it is smeared across thighs. Take turns tasting the ring pops on one another's hands—marriage tastes like cherry but also Heather's mouth before yours. Feed one another sour ropes and the nectar you make from dissolving hard candy in Sprite, bubbles eating them away. Hold your fingers up to each other's hungry mouths like a kiss, like *sorry*, like *help*.

Exhale to become a question mark to the sky—will you have me? Your head bobs on a body caving in on itself. Flat on your back, become an emptier bowl, hard as porcelain and brittle, hoping to rise to the occasion where wooden is reward. *Light as a feather, stiff as a board*, they chant fast, faster, frenzied, breath hot across your body.

At school you carry clear backpacks to show you have nothing to hide. You wear clear braces, shoes, belts as if to say there is nothing to contain. You write notes to one another with milky pens, love letters you slip between the slits in your lockers, hold breathless to your heart at recess. You live for one another's affirmations. But the plastic pens are clear to show how much ink is left, so soon it becomes best to write nothing.

In history, you are tasked with creating a presentation about the greatest invention in history. You choose refrigeration, spending long afternoons together collaging magazine cutouts of food onto an old box. You make shelves, an ice maker, spell your names in magnets across the front. When you win a pizza party, no one eats. You take turns seeing who is the smallest, who can fit inside, closing the doors like a tomb.

Light as a feather, stiff as a board, chanted in the dark strobed as your heart, stars zooming closer as you float, sway, hungry hands at your back, your waist, between your thighs.

Now your disappearance comes into view, along with your devotion. You will deliver each vanishing body throughout the night—death the only reward for little girls seeking magic.

Hug Your Mad

Mama says mad freezes your face, so little girls with feelings be careful. Anger shows ugly over time, lines between your brows or pulling down the corners of your mouth. Girls should smile, say sorry. They should hug their mad until it disappears.

Mad tastes like salt and lead, like the blood-seep of steak, rust at the bottom of the playground slide. Mad feels like gum on the bottom of your sandal, a knot in your Barbie's hair, an ant crawling up your leg, stung and swollen afterward. Sometimes mad is really bad, which girls can't be. But usually it is sad, which you feel but no one sees.

You are mad at the boy who crushes a frog with a rock at school, at your brother for eating the last of dinner when you are still hungry, at the way no one believes you when you say that lying in bed in the dark makes you feel like you will disappear. You are mad at science because you don't want to cut open a baby pig to pluck out its heart, mad at the history teacher who keeps picking you up even though he only calls on the boys in class, mad at the way you jump at the recess bell like fear is familiar. You are mad at the gym teacher telling you that basketball is for tall girls like you, mad at the math teacher saying girls can't do equations when you know that sometimes one plus one isn't two because it's something more complicated. You are mad at your name on the bad board because a boy won't stop tickling you, and the laugh is really a cry coming up out of your throat before you can catch it, swallow it silent.

Mama says mad is not a flag we wave. Hate and scared are not for sharing. When you sulk, she says the cross will mark your face. You think of her careful stitches, stabbing needle and thread through cloth to pierce out a picture. When you pull a needle through the top layer of your skin, you never bleed. You are alive and numb all at once.

"Hug your mad and it will go away," Mama singsongs. But her mad never does, no matter how she sings or sinks into a drink or onto the floor. Maybe that's why her face is lined.

You hug your mad when you correct your uncle in public, tell him a brontosaurus doesn't eat meat, and he says you're wrong and talkback isn't for girls too scared to walk in the dark hallway, too small to watch *Jurassic Park*. You walk into his embrace like a velociraptor, the smell of his too close breath too sharp.

You hug your mad when Daddy spanks you for something you didn't do, like leave the TV remote in the crack of his chair or not laugh enough at his jokes. You fetch the belt with the buckle and the cracked leather like a knuckle, waiting for the crack that signals your hurt is deserved. You know hitting is wrong, but after, you hug your mad which is really sad he thinks is bad. You cry into his shoulder.

You hug your mad when your uncles drink too much and yell when you wake them on the couch for dinner. "Sorry," you say, passing the butter and another beer. You hug your mad when your uncle goes to jail for running over his ex-wife and everyone says he didn't do it, but if he did, it was because she asked for it. You think of her creased face under his tires and your cousin watching her gasp, and how maybe you too are bad, too breathless and sad for someone to save.

You stomp your bad like a puddle, spraying mud spatter. You blow your mad into a balloon, then pop the shape. You make your sad into a companion, a lonely shadow to follow you around.

You're good at keeping secrets—like how the babysitter puts you on his lap and you don't tell, or Daddy's friend reads the back of your sweatpants real slow and says you need a boyfriend, his cigarette smoke following you down the hallway, or a stranger in the parking lot yells, "Little bitch!"

You hug your mad, but it will not disappear, like the memory of your older cousin pinning you down like butterfly Barbie, limbs splayed, face frozen. Or the way he tickles you until you can't breathe, his hands everywhere and wrong, and when you kick and cry, escape and say you want to leave, everyone says you are bad, makes you go into his room again to apologize. Hug your mad, they say, and he is waiting with his arms open to accept your sorry, tell you to smile, lock the door behind you once more.

You freeze like a doll because you don't want feelings forever on your face like your Mama and hers, women who pretend mad doesn't happen, except sometimes they can't catch their breath for no reason and sometimes you hear them scream.

You hug your mad to make it disappear, but really it is you, alive and numb all at once, a body closing in on itself, gasping for any kind of breath.

Abbreviate

We are reduced, made as small as the letters that now signify ourselves.

There are too many of us, the teachers say, to remember. We will be forgettable, they insist, if we do not change. We need to become someone else.

Sarah is a popular name in the '90s, like Gak and Koosh balls, objects for squeezing and pulling into new shapes, objects to mold for play. We understand that to be popular is to be pliable, fashioned for another's fun. We are molded each day we eat Ranch Doritos or Pizza Hut, listen to TLC on the radio, though our parents say waterfalls are not for good girls before they tell us we should not shout like Alanis, a loud girl whose name is too unusual to ever be shared.

It is true we Sarahs are many. There are five in our graduating class of approximately 60. You can throw a sticky hand or Day-Glo yo-yo and strike a Sarah without even trying. We are as common as hair scrunchies or American Girl dolls and their blank faces. We are special, our parents say, and we believe them, but then we go into the world and find out that, actually, we are not.

So we abbreviate. Now we are D and L. Some of us are Sarah and others Sara, so much changed with a single letter, teachers remind us when we miss a spelling word in English or forget to solve for Y in math. Except for names.

Now I am M, which is what the other Sarah M is too, just like we have two Sarah C's, duplicate letters more acceptable than too many Sarahs.

We aren't the only duplicates. There are too many Brittanys. Too many Brianas. All of us are too much, too many. When our names are erased, replaced with a letter, we become small like our bodies, a period at the end to signal that the decision is not ours, that we should keep quiet like when we bleed through our clothes, tie sweatshirts around our waists to hide all that we are capable of. Now the boys write R in red letters because one Briana got her period, bled red through her clothes, and they won't let her forget she has a body even though she doesn't have a name.

I liked my name before, the S like a snake's fierce head and pointed tail. The letter was brave like I never feel, the susurrus on my lips a secret or threat. I liked the symmetry, the way the name stood tall on either side, spread out wide, which I never do, a girl trained to be small from an early age, so much so that after a while my spine learns to curve in on itself.

On the first day each year, we drew our names on tags, and I watched Sarah spread out and out. I colored the cursive green like vines winding through time and flowering like I hope I might do once middle school is over, like how maybe I could be as pretty as the girls on TV, girls with unique names like Cordelia and Willow. But now I'm just an initial. I color my M in red, like *stop* or *sorry* or *shame*.

Next to me a girl is crying when she colors because Anna is not her name, but the teacher says he won't remember Annayelli, couldn't pronounce it even if he wanted to, though white boys with made-up names are easy to remember and spell.

Anna and I pass red and purple crayons back and forth, handing them to the C's and D's behind us until the names that aren't ours look like a bruise, like a wound.

I try to be M. I draw it tall as mountains, pointed on each end like impressive peaks. I try to like M by making it one half of a crown, a bird flying somewhere better, a lightning bolt. I try to make it sharp as teeth, the kind of letter that would shout, "M is not my name and if it is too hard to remember multiples exist, then why are all the books we read by men named Dave, why is every president named Bush, and why do you expect me to remember all three teachers named Smith?"

There is the Smith that teaches Spanish and the Smith that surfs and teaches history and the Smith that is the principal until he runs off with a student who was just a letter too, except he thought she was something special.

Sarah is a snake with a sharp tongue but M is a mumble. I don't know M when the teacher calls—I need to remember this is me now. After a while of not knowing myself, I learn not to say anything, just like I learn not to raise my hand in science or history because girls are never expected to know the correct answer. After a while, I become M, looking down at my feet instead of up at the stars.

My best friend does not think this is right. She holds me when I feel invisible and says I deserve to be special. I blush when she insists on calling me by both my first and middle names, Sarah Fawn. She introduces me to others this way as if the names were always meant to be together like Mary Ann. She will not accept my smallness, demands instead that I become more, become mythic, both girl and creature, something magic. She will do this in middle school, in high school, in college and beyond, until her loving name for me becomes the name I claim.

Still, in school I am M in class and on the board. M is all curves when the teacher draws it. The boys point out that it looks like a pair of boobs, and they sneak nipples on the top when we head out to recess, watching my face go red when we return. The joke is that I haven't got any, not like the D who has a name to match her chest size. She's fat, everyone says, belly like the letter, but she wears a bra with good straps for snapping, and the boys can throw chips down her shirt to watch her dig them out.

We are best friends, D and M, just like H and the other M. L tags along with the Brittanys, K and C. Sometimes we hang out with the Jessicas, who get to be their real names because one is Japanese and the other is Black. They're the only diversity at our rural school until the parents decide to bring in exchange students so we'll have things to write about in our college essays, except they only allow European students from countries that speak English. Everyone likes to say the Jessicas are only half anyway.

If you are all anything—like Black James—you get a nickname to match, one that says what you are, especially if you are the only one in the school. Black James makes a joke that he is special like a Power Ranger or licorice, but he flinches when teachers make him stand for the Pledge of Allegiance or to play Christmas songs in band because he is the only Jehovah's Witness too.

"Everyone has to be the same," the teachers say, sameness good for everything but names.

When we play in band, the flutes are too soft because Briana disappeared when the teasing would not. Black James moves his trombone's slide in time with the others, holds his mouth to look the same, but it is obvious he is the only Black student, and he doesn't actually make a sound.

There are many Bens and Lees and Jesses, but this is fine because one is the quarterback and the other a receiver, one a goalie and the other a starting forward. One Matt does FFA and raises pigs for slaughter, another Matt skateboards and has a lisp, which is why the teachers would never call him S, and one plays guitar loud at all the pep rallies while Black James only pretends.

Boys are not letters. They are too big to take up such a small space, which is why they are called by their last names. They are Thomas and Ross and Squires. They are last names just like the teachers, just like the coaches. Just like they are something special.

The only time boys are letters are when they are wearing their letterman jackets, embroidered with a green T for our town, for our school. From our place at the sidelines, we abbreviate, watch them run and score and win. Their jackets flash green T's like go, go fast, go ahead, go when and wherever you want.

Skip It

We risk tripping because girlhood demands injury.

First we learn to jump rope, arcing the cord overhead like the boys playing tetherball, swinging the rope to loop like a noose around the pole they tell us to dance on, or like our father's belts when we are bad, though in this game we can escape the hurt if we are quick and small enough.

We hold our breaths and lift off the ground like hollow-boned birds, too-big hearts for such small bodies, hovering for a moment before coming down.

Sometimes we fall, like when we forget to expel the air from our bodies before we hold rigid as corpses, hovering like ghosts, or when we look foolish at our feet. Soaring means air out, eyes up, means flee somewhere else, surrender.

Girls learn jump rope while boys learn soccer. We are taught to hold still for success, to go up but only so high, while the boys learn to play the field, to score and celebrate. We learn to trip, a lifetime of falling.

At recess we practice. We fall in love with the boys who force us to kiss them while the others jeer. We fall for each other, stuffing love letters between the slits in our lockers, declaring breathless that no one understands what it means to want to disappear. We fall into each other's arms to discover trust is never guaranteed. If we are small and pretty as waifs we are caught and admired; if we are not, we learn letting go is punishment, never pleasure.

Now Toys "R" Us says fun is skipping, tripping. We each have one—a Skip It around our ankle like a shackle. We place our foot inside during each lunch and recess, swinging our leg to set the spiral in motion.

The game is to jump over the self-imposed hurtle each time it swings back around forever or fall.

More than one girl loses a tooth, bloodies palms with her carelessness. Breonna is too clumsy, can't keep up, her front teeth jutting from her lips so she never smiles. Savannah is too afraid to leap, limps and lisps away like in class when her tongue won't cooperate and the boys point until she goes silent. Becky is too clumsy and cries out quit. So many of us learn to give up before the bell even rings.

For fun we try to outrun pain even though we are standing still. We jump and jump, trying to reach infinity. The spiral only stops when we do. The way we are learning to avoid hurt is to keep going forever.

We gather in a circle around each successful girl like a shrine, watching sweat shine on her brow, red and pained, her eyes to the skies. We count how long she can avoid the inevitable. There is no need—the Skip It clicks each successful rotation, marking accomplishment like miles on a treadmill or calories on a wrapper, the tally scores some of us have started cutting on our arms and thighs.

We skip snacks to jump, leave our lunch to leap. Like our mothers and theirs, we must be small to be a success. We skip secrets like how Meghan lets the history teacher dance with her sometimes, or Dawn's dad bruises her body. Each failure is a reason to prove ourselves again. We when trip—over feet and feelings—we reset the counter. We start back at zero.

The lesson is obsession, one we cannot forget these many years later, still braced for a lifetime of falling.

We learn to leap without looking, to accept injury as part of the game. Juicy Jackie shows her breasts to the boys for money to go to medical school until her brother steals the bank. Tiny Tori wins first prize in the horse jumping show but breaks her brittle bones and spends a summer in a cast looking up from her bed at all those blue ribbons. Eventually, Angela jumps her car off a cliff when her boyfriend leaves her, and so does Tanya a decade later, driving over a cliff into the sea, convinced—for just a moment—she can fly.

Brittany falls best, into bed with a hundred men and a camera, beautiful and breathless onscreen, her eyes to the skies just like we learned.

Connect the Dots Love

N says we're looking for that Leo and Kate love that crashes sudden, veins fire and ice, the kind where you go down with the ship.

I tell N that Kate didn't die, except inside, but N doesn't mind because she's lusting after Leo while I'm trying not to stare at Kate's pale bobbing breasts. I wonder how he can concentrate enough to draw her with a steady hand, to make a solid line. Her skin's like N's, translucent moon and swoon.

We lie out in the sun to burn, trying so hard to be golden that even our skin peels away from us. We talk sky (good) and sea (better) and how to breathe in a circle to make the music last.

We're listening to the Spice Girls say what they really, really want, and N shows me how to be two ways at once—breathing in even as you exhale. "The note won't break," she says, fingering her imaginary clarinet. "No one knows when you're struggling for air."

I can't keep up. I'm always spurting out staccato, gasping where I begin, choking when I end.

N touches my throat, my stomach. We practice breathing together like the afternoon never stops.

Maybe love is Leo letting go, the way he freezes when the hurt is too good. N swears he's ro-man-tic, stretching out the middle like her want, gender a pulse in her throat. Her hand grasps mine during sleepover movies when an asteroid heads toward Earth or the poltergeist comes through the television.

It feels like everything is always dying—my breath on my tongue, the small fish of N's foot in my lap when Ben saunters by, the smell of vanilla body spray we waltz through before the school dance where we slam our bodies down and wind them all around.

Ben grabs my waist and later N cries because she has no one to dance with but me.

"Connect the dots," N says into the mirror while I bring her Dr. Pepper Lip Smackers to my lips like a kiss. "You don't count."

With the lights out and the glow-in-the-dark bracelets we wave through the gym, I am a specter, my lonely lit up for the world to see.

In band, N taps my thigh to keep time. I struggle to keep up, the sound my instrument makes a strangle. It's better not to make noise, I think. Since I'm always behind, it's better not to breathe at all.

In science I label the parts of a jellyfish—the tentacles, the arms that capture prey and ingest them with poisonous venom but that also pull desire up into the mouth hidden hungry in the center of the creature. They pulse and billow like ghosts, gorgeous if they want, invisible if they need.

I remind N that the Titanic didn't sink that deep, instead became a reef. Jellyfish dance through the ballroom, stand on the railing, arms out and flying.

But N isn't interested in the wreckage, just the wreck. She wants that romance where someone loves you because they leave. Where you know you were special because someone haunts you the rest of your life.

Constellate

They shout when the small moon of my fist orbits her spine, my hurt lined red across her skin, her shins rubbed raw on the carpeted high school hallway. She leaves a Pluto-blue bruise with a well-aimed kick to my hip, and with her arm across my throat, I smell her musk and the sweet heat of her breath and Victoria's Secret Love Spell, the way we all smell, like belonging is sorcery written in the stars. With her face close to mine, I see Saturn ringing her eye from the last fight.

In high school, we fight every day after lunch where we share orange slices and diet tips and Tylenol for the cramps confining us. We cuddle and brush each other's hair and talk about the lonely that comes even when you're with a crowd, which is why we constellate our collective hurt, wrestling to see how strong we are, because Tasha stopped eating last month and Becky's dad says she was an accident and Teresa wants Kelly but that isn't allowed, just like we're not allowed to show a bra strap or say we don't believe in God even though it's hard to believe in a higher power when the middle school principal ran off with a student from his church whose underwear showed all the time.

Sometimes our ass shows from beneath our shorts, or a nipple, but bodies are ok if they are hurting, and no one says stop, not even the teachers, who gather like gravity to watch. They place bets, shout, "Fight, girl," gender an asteroid in their throats like how the pregnant girls are expelled or Julie is a slut for dating the band teacher before she graduates or how everyone calls Taylor a girl until he shoots himself in the head and then he becomes a man.

When the boys fight, shoving each other into lockers or shouting "pussy" across the quad, they are pulled apart and whisked away, but when we fight each day—even the days we weren't planning but the crowd shows anyway—everyone laughs at the girls eclipsed by fists, the girls who've waned all light-year until our pants hang from the comets of our hips.

At night we stand naked, pale as moons in front of our mirrors. We pulse the tender points, the bruises, the scabs, the places where our dearest have left their hurt so we might feast, though our mouths are sore from being wire-trapped into precision and the effort of keeping silent.

We are not lonely then, our collective hurt scattered and shining across the galaxies of our bodies. We count our bruises blessings, proof that somebody loves us. We feel, for a moment, like we could be something to wish on.

Lights, Camera, Action

On-screen we are buried alive. We rest like corpses under soil, tombstones at our heads. We close our eyes tight, feeling the weight of earth over our faces. Stealing small sips of air from holes left for us to breathe, we lie still as the dead and wait for the director to yell, "Action!"

Then we rise and lumber slowly toward the boys behind the camera like zombies. We are only in high school, but already we know that dead is the best way for a girl to get noticed.

We've grown up when being captured on-screen is still a novelty. We subsist on disposable cameras, cardboard boxes full of film whose photos turn out blurry and spectral. We feel the same—disposable, unpretty and unloved, braces glinting as our breasts refuse to grow, acne scattering feral across our faces. Still, we put on a show. We know girlhood is a performance, womanhood even more so.

Our lives are carefully crafted. Offstage we are insecure, but confidence is a costume we put on like music at a sleepover, frosted eyeshadow or glossy lips, dimming the overheads so we glow ghoulish under a black light, winding our hips like snakes or the women we see on MTV. We pose eager for the camera, but the photos we develop are never what we imagine we look like, the harsh flash illuminating our faces pale as ghosts, our pouting mouths open and afraid.

We are desperate to be loved, so we are desperate to be captured, even if only on camera. A few of our classmates have camcorders, and there are more in the video production classroom. Even our teachers are eager to allow video projects to break up the monotony of paper assignments. So we make history projects in groups divided along predictable gender lines. We girls are not allowed to participate in elaborate World War II scenes featuring paintball guns and smoke grenades, must instead play docile housewives succumbing to classmate harassment because this is what our teacher says is historically accurate. We agree to wear straitjackets for a filmed talent show skit, then dance onstage in front of our school following directions from male classmates who direct us to act crazy.

We film scenes from Shakespeare plays where women are the wittiest but the men don't realize. We roll our eyes at one another when our male classmates can't deliver the lines because they don't understand the jokes. We would rather kiss each other during *Romeo and Juliet*, soft bubblegum tongues and smiles cherry sweet, hands around the crescent slivers of skin revealed by our low-rise jeans, but this is something we hide from ourselves, let alone the sharp focus of a camera or a television in a darkened classroom.

We learn what we have always known—we are not allowed to be who we imagine ourselves to be with someone else directing. We do not want to be dead, do not want to be wives. We do not want to stand in front of the camera while our male classmates insist on moving us around like dolls or costumed props because they have claimed the roles of director or executive producer. We are tired of standing around watching them dismiss our ideas for hours until the sun goes down and they announce with dramatic flourish that we've lost the light.

So we claim a stage of our own. We make our own movies after school and on weekends, claiming visibility on screens no one will see. We wander through the woods in search of witches, fog on our breaths and bramble at our backs. We craft elaborate musicals set to our favorite songs, filming early in the morning when no one will see us dancing and laughing in real life.

Sometimes we just film each other. We film each other spinning in sunlight. We capture close-ups of freckles across someone's thigh. We find the right light to cast shadows in the cupid's bow above someone's full lips. We tangle together in the grass, imagining, unclear where one body ends and another begins.

One day, we film a tour of the galaxy. We craft elaborate papier-mâché planets as big as our small bodies, painting them in swirling watercolor, affixing them to the garage ceiling with invisible string. We hang black curtains to create the vastness of space, using a hole punch to create constellations we thread through with white and purple twinkle lights. We shine flashlights to illuminate the planetary bodies and our own. On camera, you can see us whispering in the cosmos, guiding each other through the unknown.

Then, an interruption. A boy from school suddenly appears and pulls one of us by the hand into a darkened bedroom.

"Wait for me," she calls, so as not to be left out of the action. But she never returns.

More than one of us will pursue moviemaking. More than one of us will go to film school believing a college degree will guarantee success and immortalization on-screen. More than one of us will move to L.A. and live in a crappy apartment underneath the Hollywood sign, listening to sirens wailing throughout the night. One of us will even marry, then divorce, a mediocre actor from a famous family, though this mostly means she does odd jobs on the set while he gets the billing, much the way we remember our youth, sitting on high school sets while our boyfriends asked us to fetch them something to drink while they cast other women to kiss.

No one makes it, really. Except the girl pulled from the heavens by some boy bored enough to interrupt our girlish fun, to tell the whole school about it later, to say she wasn't really that good after all.

Just after graduation, when we are mostly miserable but still posing happy on the Internet, she makes one professional film, then another. Soon her extensive filmography is available on the Internet, if you know where to look.

I watch. A few times. She is still beautiful underneath who she is pretending to be. She has a stage name, something feminine and sexual. She has dyed her hair, gotten implants and injections, dolled herself up to match the poorly scripted lines she moans. She is kissing all the girls like we always wanted but never could, though this, too, is performance.

It is hard to look away from her, naked and exposed, frightened and desperate. She looks like we all did so many years ago, buried by others alive on-screen, lying still as the dead until the director yells, "Action!" and she begins gasping for breath.

Unreliable Narrator

Never trust a woman who does not trust herself.

I learn this in college. In literature, women are too untrustworthy to see beyond their own pride to realize at first that they should marry the wealthy man who is supposed to be swoonworthy but mostly seems boring. They are young women who move to New York City only to find themselves in the mad eye of a hurricane of their own making. I like these women, but we only analyze their faults.

In class, no one believes a woman who raises her hand, uncertain, to answer a question or who whispers something to the teacher when called on unprompted. "What makes you think so?" professors ask, teaching us how to read closely but also that a woman's opinion should always bear the burden of proof. "Support your answer." We learn hesitation more than certainty.

In bars, no one believes a woman who says she is not interested in a free drink, in a dance, a phone number, a ride home. "Prove it," sweaty men say, hovering so close you can smell alcohol in their pores, a challenge on their breath. "You know you want it." Sometimes we accept whatever is offered just to make the attention go away.

At home no one believes a woman who says she is frightened by the boys and men in her own family. I am expected to smile and hug boys and men I have seen strike women, children, and animals long after I am an adult and no one is supposed to tell me what to do. Male family members drink too much and share stories about punching women in the past and also recently, plus all the queers who had it coming. Male family friends comment on my body, laughing when I rise to anger, scolding me later for acting so cold. "You're overreacting," they say. "Don't be so sensitive." Eventually, I believe them, believe myself suspicious.

Actually, never trust a woman who does not trust the men around her.

I learn this in college. In literature, women who do not trust their husbands are locked away in the attic, wailing and miserable, haunting their own lives. Women who do not accept their roles as happy wives and mothers wander aimless to drown in the sea. Though I know better than to praise them in papers, I like these women most.

In class, professors insist group work should be completed by groups of men and women, acting as though it does not matter that the men refuse to take notes, to attend meetings, to do little more than read prepared PowerPoint slides for the presentation. "That's how groups work," they say to complaints, as if learning to accept this is part of the assignment. Soon I deceive myself into believing this is right.

At bars, the men I am dating count the calories in my drinks and say my dress is too short, and the men I am not dating buy me unwanted double shots and try to lift up my skirt on the dance floor. When I only want to dance with women, I am not trying hard enough to find a man, I am too closed off, I will never be happy. This feels untrue, but I will myself to believe it anyway. Eventually, I no longer know who is telling the story.

At home, my college roommate says she was sexually assaulted by a classmate during a group project. The work is not done, and the professor will make no exceptions, so the boy comes to our house while they are finishing the project and assaults me too.

Perhaps the story is never trust a woman who does not know what trust—what truth—even is.

I learn this in college. I try to write literature where the woman is me, where I tell all the stories no one has ever believed. There is the story of a woman who was assaulted by a man over and over, though she never reported it because who would believe that she didn't deserve it, who would believe that she was foolish enough to allow it to happen, and more than once? There is the story of a young woman whose first boyfriend told her she was too big when she felt too small, and she was happy when she was sad, and perhaps she did not know her own mind as well as he did. There is a story of a little girl who tries to tell the adults true stories about monsters but they insist she is telling stories, imagining again.

In class, I learn about philosophy and politics, places where truth is absolute according to the men who write history. I memorize the answers expected of me to earn A's and escape male professors who sleep with students so secretly it doesn't seem real, so often it seems normal. They rarely lose credibility.

In bars, we toast as one by one, my friends find men, find out they are bad, find ways to excuse this behavior, get married. I attend celebrations I do not believe to be joyful, but I am so good at smiling. I am so good at saying, "Congratulations" and meaning it. I am so good at lying that I even convince myself.

At home, alone, doubt is my favorite game. I wonder if memory is a snake shedding its skin to become something new. I wonder if truth is a star that eventually burns out. I wonder if a woman is a fact or a fiction. I stand a long time in front of the stranger that is me in the mirror trying to decide.

Fair

From our swaying seats at the top of the Ferris wheel, we witness the entire small town. There is the gas station with the best Big Gulps, and there is the empty lot where we used to meet before piling into the car of whoever had the most gas. There is the coffee shop we decided to like when we become adults, and there is the freeway that cuts through town like a vein pulsing someplace better, the one we use to drive to the new lives we've made after we left the place we can't help but come back to.

We return every summer to visit our families and the ghosts of who we once were. We have ridden the Ferris wheel every year, every decade, our lives—like our mothers' and theirs—an endless cycle around a fixed position like planets around the sun.

Now I am trapped in a metal cage with my friend and the man who has trapped her in a life neither of us recognize. She asks his permission to go on the ride. She asks his permission to eat a funnel cake. She asks his permission to play carnival games where she wins nothing but unsolicited advice about how to throw balls into bowls of cowering fish or aim darts at shining balloons. She asks his permission to purchase souvenirs with her own money.

On the ride, he swings the cage back and forth in the air, laughing at my fear, the way I hold my breath before the fall. Down below, the ride operator shouts to hold still, and the man asks, "What does he know?" though it is clear we are not supposed to answer the question.

My friend—another Sarah from the '90s, so many of us growing up with the same name and set of expectations—asks him to put his arm around her. He tells her there is not enough room, which means he thinks she's too fat despite a lifetime of dieting, our elementary play punctuated with her Weight Watchers meetings and doctor's appointments, her ejection from recess sports for being too slow or afterschool clubs for being uncool.

"It's not fair," she used to cry, motioning to her body, then mine.

"That's cool," she says now, but clearly it is not, and she shifts in her seat so as to appear smaller, which is unnecessary since she already takes up so little of seat. The man she met online, the one who lives with her rent-free and is still looking for a job, who complains that she is too busy finishing college and working full-time to clean their apartment, spreads his legs so wide that she must sit at an angle. I am forced to stare directly at his crotch.

I am tired of being shaken in the air. I am tired of being laughed at by a man who cannot take a joke, raising his voice at our girlish fun, a stranger expecting me to follow his orders like he's my father. I am tired of being afraid—of falling, of my friend's future, of my own because, really, he is not so different from the men I date.

Down we go, heading toward Earth before rising again to meet the stars. I can see my past illuminated. There is the fake mountain built of concrete we used to climb as children. Our mothers would leave us on one side, and we would feel brave climbing the built-in steps through the craggy surface, holding our arms wide when we reached the top, which is noticeably shorter now that I've aged, perhaps just a story or two. I remember delighting in the fear of being on our own, me and my other Sarah, both of us brave only because we were together.

There is my favorite roller coaster, the one shaped like a dragon plummeting through the darkness. It is too small for adults, but I remember how we rode as children, our bodies pressing against one another as we took the sharp turns.

There are the fair animals, blue-ribbon pigs and sheep, glossy chickens looking for their food. There are Clydesdale horses like in the commercials for the Budweiser her boyfriend has been pounding all night and cows branded with the names of wealthy men in town. These were my favorite as a child, but now I recognize them as animals trapped for slaughter.

I spy the fortune teller's rickety booth adorned with filmy scarves and purple lights. As girls, we could never afford for her to read our palms or gaze into her clouded crystal ball to tell us if we might be fortunate enough to be someone's crush. Instead, we made our own magic, elaborately folded paper cootie catchers to tell us which boys in school might be ours, where we might get married, how many children we would have, how many rooms we would clean in our house, girlhood play the practice for a lifetime of labor.

Now we are old enough to pay for the chance to learn the direction of our lives, though my friend will likely to need to ask permission. I wonder what the fortuneteller knows. I wonder if our futures are fair. I wonder if she knows the secrets my Sarah and I do not share. How I am running from a man who hurt me. How she is running to a man who will hurt her. How in the future our bodies will flinch in instinctive fear when a man raises his voice, because we will remember a raised fist. How we will know this is not fair and still we will accept another ride with the same kind of man, orbiting the same fixed point again and again. How after a lifetime of loving one another, we will separate, just drift away like the fair when it packs up and leaves town, because it is too hard to share the ways we are broken.

The sounds of the fair fill the night sky. The jingle of rides, the clanging bells of someone winning an oversized prize, children laughing or begging for more cotton candy. From the competing concert venues, one band croons a country song about a wandering woman and a classic rock musician wails about a beautiful girl desperate to run away. Though we do not speak, I can hear my friend's loneliness because it is my own.

Round and round we go, cycling through time, neon and glowing. It feels like we are flying. And then we come down.

Mystery House

A door opens onto a wall. A window is trapped behind another.

I visit the mystery house with my college boyfriend for an anniversary, but really, I am trying to uncover how I became a girl who accepts being torn down and rebuilt like this house. I am looking to solve the riddle where one and one do not make two but rather one is greater than the other, my world easily absorbed by a boy who says he loves me but does not want me to love anything else. Even myself.

I have been to the Winchester Mystery House before, on a high school trip, shrouded in another life. Back then, we wandered the 160 rooms, learned about the 10,000 windows and 2,000 doors, and though most laughed at a widowed woman so mad she devoted her life to building a labyrinth around herself, already I understood trying to create something that would keep you unreachable and free.

My high school friends and I kept each other close as lovers, whispered secret devotions and smoothed our hands over one another's bodies to tend to what haunted us. There was the friend who was secretly dating a teacher, sneaking into his room on nights he was supposedly our chaperone. He knew we knew, and during the day he scolded us for giggling or straying off the path. There was the friend who gave herself to any boy who would have her because her father said she was conceived to replace a dead sister. There was the friend who threw up after every meal. The friend who cut herself to feel. The friend who hated herself because she hated a girl loving a girl.

How I loved them, these girls. We grew up playing doctor, trying to heal hurts no one would see or believe, and with my oversized dollhouse, taking turns shimmying our growing bodies out the front door as if trying to escape. But after graduation, we saw each other rarely, as memories, as ghosts on the Internet. We tried to flee, but mostly we moved our hurts somewhere else as we built new homes.

I have tried to build a home with my college boyfriend. He says the woman who built the mystery house must be haunted. He says the same about me, when I have feelings he does not understand, mostly unhappy ones about our relationship, or when I do not want to do whatever he desires like shoot guns or play video games or listen to him incorrectly correct me. Or mend a fight that he started by giving him my body.

He does not like my body anyway, monitors what I eat by tracking calories on a sheet of paper he keeps in his pocket or removing my plate from in front of me during a meal. One Valentine's Day, he buys me a chocolate cake in the shape of a heart and permits me one piece before throwing the rest away. As the years add up, pounds subtract on the scale and people ask me where I've vanished.

At its most expansive, the mystery house had hundreds more rooms. Now many are lost, crumbled, walled off, or inaccessible. I imagine them as holes on the inside, wounds that will never be healed because they cannot be reached.

I wander toward another of the six kitchens, but my boyfriend reaches for my hand to pull me back in his direction. The tour guide talks about legends, stories about spirits and superstitions. Most are made up, a convenient way for others to understand a difficult woman.

But it is no mystery to me why a woman would want to wall herself in, would build something only to watch it fail and be forced to begin again.

It will be many years before I leave him in order to build something of my own.

For now, we take the stairs. He climbs the conventional ones, moves easily to another floor. I prefer to take the ones where you climb and climb, convinced you might be mad, might be hovering between life and death, claustrophobic in the tiny corridor, the walls closing in, all that time and effort only to move a few feet, to go nowhere.

Dash

At dusk the light goes diffuse, like slow motion, like simple. The backyard trees are velvet; cirrus swift brushstrokes make the sky seem safe. The railroad rattling through the front yard slows too, whistle filtered through the gloaming until it sounds like a dream.

My mother escapes the confines of the house this time each day to circle the yard alone. She is careful to avoid the toys that litter the yard—a broken bicycle, a shattered sand pail, a naked doll whose eyes are scratched carefully to blank. Lately, she spies homemade pipes.

She steps slow in this strange landscape she calls home, where her sons throw punches instead of baseballs, where she sleeps with her door locked.

She walks barefoot to feel the reassurance of earth, the reminder she is solid.

Now and then she gathers rocks for each life loan defaulted, another bill unpaid, another son's arrest, disappointment piled high on the table where the good meat should glisten. Most of her many children are gone, motherhood a lifetime of small miracles and abandonments. She cups pebbles the size of pennies in her calloused hands, palming them like worry stones.

It is painful to look down for too long—broken toys like the breaking bodies of her children, the grass long dead with the California drought—so she keeps her eyes to the skies.

She grew up looking down —walking on stars, Hollywood lit up eternal on the hill. Learned walking over others was the way. Now she is stooped like the mark of a question she forgot to ask, spends her evenings filling her pockets just to empty them all over again.

At dusk she walks with her head held up, hair falling back to reveal the lines around her lips, the ways she is marked by a lifetime of shutting her mouth.

She breathes in the evening cooling down the summer heat, and the scent of the lilacs, that strong sweetness at the back of the throat. The blooms return each spring no matter how the family has changed, her boys smoking, snorting whatever they can find.

She can hear the television inside turned up to full volume for her husband, the news blaring the latest disaster, earthquake, tornado, rising tides, the state on fire. She can hear her sons fighting inside, the ones who haven't left yet echoing the violence of the ones already gone, the sound of a fist against a wall, the dark constellations they leave in the wake of their frustrations.

The stars are just appearing, bright pinpricks in the sky. They look like sugar scattered across a table, sweetness overhead when down here she mostly tongues tears.

She feeds herself instead on the ritual— harvesting rock where nothing grows, California dry as a scab plucked from a wound. Her body, too, a constellation of scars.

She lives for the moment when day shifts to night, that imperceptible in-between. She has always lived on the ground and among the stars all at once. She is always waiting for leaving's arrival.

Bats are only visible in this in-between, so she escapes her life each night to watch time separate in their flight. She creates something living from what is dead, pretends pebbles are insects as she tosses them upward for the creatures that emerge to feast each evening.

Arcing stones in the dark, she watches what seems as if it should live on land take to the sky. Bats dash, compelled by the chance for flesh, to suck blood from a stone.

Flight Pattern

How we climb before the fall. The swift ascent moves the airplane toward the moon, the stars, something bigger than ourselves, if only we would notice. All around, cold cabin air repressurizes so our bodies never realize how close we are to chaos.

I fly home exhausted from work travel and the tension of living in a timeline where the world seems to burst into flames each day anew, doomscrolling a hobby like posing happy for strangers on the Internet or side hustling because even a good job does not provide enough pay.

I twist my body into a small seat, glancing across the aisle to see a mother struggling to fit even her young children into the allotted space. Up front, passengers who can afford the luxury of room stretch their feet and raise their arms for glasses of complementary champagne. We spy them between curtains drawn to create a barrier between our ways of life. I walk past upon entering, men in dark business suits staring openly, sometimes winking or smiling at me while I wait my turn to file to the back of the plane, moving around their shiny loafers and briefcases.

I avert my eyes, looking down, shuffling slowly to my seat where I hope I will become invisible enough that some strange man does not try to buy me a drink, does not spend the flight talking about his very important job or his very miserable children, inching closer into my space by pretending to care about the book I am reading or writing, until at last he can ask for my phone number, me trapped in the middle seat, unable to leave, unable to simply say, "No."

Sometimes it is easier to pretend to be asleep, but when I have done this in the past, men have repositioned their legs to tangle with mine, have attempted to pull me to rest on their shoulders, have placed their hands over mine on the armrest, which is the most generous sharing of the space I usually receive. It is hard to pretend to fall asleep but harder still to pretend to wake, to be the one to apologize for their behavior and then sit stone-faced for the rest of the flight.

Once, a married man talked to me for the duration of a long, bumpy flight, reaching his hand toward mine when I told him I was traveling across the country for a job interview, his thigh firmly against mine, feigning support until flight attendants announced an emergency landing. Then he called them over to berate them for inconveniencing his return home to his wife after a business trip, leaning across my lap as though I were in silent agreement before unfastening his seatbelt, straddling me without asking me to move, and marching firmly to the cockpit where he demanded to speak to the pilots. He flashed a smile when he climbed over me once more, his belt buckle at my face, and told me, "You're welcome."

Tonight I am grateful to have paid extra for an aisle seat, for the absence it affords on a least one side of me. Across the aisle, the woman has managed to coax her children into sleep, and we make brief, exhausted eye contact before the cabin lights go dark and the city lights are visible out the windows, billboards for clothing and medications that will make you look and feel younger, advertisements for political candidates who openly say they do not respect women but would like our votes anyway.

Just before the cabin doors close, an angry man and his sad wife and his crying infant board the plane and sit beside me. I know he is angry because he mutters to his wife that he fucking hates the middle seat, and I know she is sad because he makes her hold the crying infant and his computer and his snacks and his red trucker hat and his camo backpack and his camo blanket and camo pillow, though they do little to disguise this kind of man. He tells his wife to lean against the window with the baby so he can claim her armrest. Then he uses his shoulder to swiftly shove my arm off the back of our shared space.

I am stunned into silence. I am angry and a little afraid. I stuff these feelings into the overhead compartment.

Throughout the flight the man acts like so many men in this country preparing for takeoff. He grows restless in his seat. He sighs audibly so others will know his frustration. He picks a fight with his wife. He will not hold his infant daughter. He corrects the flight attendant. He says, "Calm down," though it is unclear which woman he is commanding.

He reaches his foot under my seat to kick my bag out of his way and my feet into the aisle so he can stretch as wide as possible.

He looks at my phone screen where I am reading *The New York Times* presidential election coverage and says loudly, "Someone thinks she's fancy," before announcing the female candidate is a bitch. He says the same about me to his wife. He says the same to me when I attempt to share the armrest again. This time he uses his elbow to ram into my arm.

I freeze. Afraid, I cannot seem to move. Then I decide I will not move.

He elbows me harder. Harder. He reaches across the armrest into my seat and jams his elbow again and again into my soft side. Later, I will find bruises across my pale moon flesh.

I tell no one of the casual violence. This is a full flight. Where will I go?

I look across the aisle and out the window. I see a vast empty sky. I cannot find a star, see instead another plane leaving a fiery rocket path across the heavens, blazing hot and angry toward the future.

When we land, the man gives me a few more shoves. He tries to talk to me through my headphones. He shouts, "Bitch!" at my back while we walk through the terminal. He matches my quickened pace. Soon I am running. No one stops to help me, afraid of their own conflict with this man, this America.

The only thing that silences him is when I fly into the open arms of my waiting husband.

Excuse Me

"Excuse me," you say when a stranger walks into your body on the sidewalk. You sensed the inevitable collision, shifted your stride to avoid his inattention, even stepped down into the dirty gutter a few times, soiling your shoes, and still the force of his shoulder stuns you.

"Excuse me," you say at work, when male colleagues or random students bump into you in crowded hallways or outside where the grass and sidewalk stretch endlessly in the collegiate autumn sun, your shadow stretching ahead as if trying to escape.

Sometimes you get angry and mutter, "Excuse you," or, "Hey." Sometimes you are honest and whimper, "Ow." But you know better.

You know it doesn't matter what you say, your words, like your body, not of much worth. It is foolish to assume you warrant the same attention as whatever is displayed on a phone screen during someone's latest doomscroll, or that you deserve the same space as a businessman's briefcase. You are no match for a man blaring music from his phone, ordering a coffee, even throwing away trash at the park, your body as disposable there next to the rusted can.

If it is rare you speak up, it is rarer still someone listens. If they do, you are rewarded with crossed arms or aggressive steps closer after you have said something about the man claiming the entire shared plane armrest or walking directly into you despite your obvious attempts at dodging interaction. You are rewarded with silence or laughter when you express anger or fear when a man has deliberately touched you, grabbed you on escalators or subways, at crowded concerts or shopping centers.

Once, in a grocery store, you expressed frustration after a man brushed up against you in the produce, water from the overhead misters the only thing separating your body from his. Then he followed you around the store until—panicked—you attempted to flee. You tried to quickly pay the cashier, who did not understand the distress and smiled when the man crept up behind you once more, grabbing your shoulder as though he had not sensed your fear during the chase.

"Aren't you going to give me your number?" he asked.

"Go on, honey," someone else said, the rest of the checkout line murmuring as if this were the sweetest thing in the world.

Once, at a funeral, an elderly man stood behind the circle of weeping family members and grabbed your ass. When you turned to utter something nonsensical, he winked, sipped his drink, and walked away. Later, you spoke up again to tell someone what he had done. "You must have imagined it," they said, as though your complaint was ruining the event.

So you apologize. You say it to others, but it is really for yourself. You are sorry for not speaking up when a man backs into you in a store aisle, for not claiming space when a man stands so close behind you at a concert you can feel his erection, for allowing your body to be so easily dismissed by the man who runs into you in a park and sighs, "Calm down, lady," when you react.

You wonder when your body ceased to matter. As a girl, you were praised for sitting quietly, for crossing your legs, for folding your hands in your lap like a scared animal. You were praised for holding still when the doctor applied a cast to your broken arm after a boy pushed you too hard during a game of tag you weren't even playing. You were praised when your arm ached and still you fluttered the heavy cast ever so gently in Swan Lake, a wounded thing trying to fly.

Boys in elementary school would jump cleanly through hopscotch squares, could make sure they did not step on a crack so as not to break their mothers' backs, but you may as well have been the chalk outline around bodies traced on the asphalt, later smudged under everyone's shoes. How they loved to shove your desk with their own, lurching you backward and forward during class so the teacher would turn and scold you for taking up so much space. How they loved to push you off of the swing to claim it for their own or go down the slide too quickly in order to frighten you, kicking you from behind.

Sure, your body was praised sometimes, some panting middle school boy desperate for your affection. But it was always for the gap between your thighs, the hollow in your neck, the way your jutting hipbones held your low-rise jeans away from your body so others could peer down your pants. You were only noticed when you disappeared, and this attention was contingent upon your returned adoration, on giving whatever was left of yourself to whoever wanted to claim it.

Later, you became a burden. High school football players shoved you and your marching band uniform out of the way on game days. Your male classmates pretended not see you in line for lunch, convinced their hunger overshadowed your own. In college, a man walking into you was supposed to be clumsy flirtation, the same as a hand accidentally on your breast or your waist, accidentally pulling you into laps or onto a couch. Once, at a bar, you watched two men pointing at you in the crowd and discussing while they laughed. You were walking, and suddenly one of them bumped you into the outstretched arms of another, who tried to dip you low for a kiss.

How you wish you'd left this behavior in your youth. But your friend's husband bumped you in the kitchen while he helped his wife make dinner. And your adult brothers claimed all the space at the family table. Your old college friend walked into you on a trip and then told you to hold his sunglasses and phone in your purse.

Another picked you up without your permission as though you were a girl again.

A waiter bringing food to your table knocked your leg, and another waiter bringing food to another table pushed the back of your chair. The dentist scooted his chair too close to yours and you felt the collision in your mouth. The realtor selling you a home used his arm to push you aside in his efforts to catch up with your husband.

Over time your body has learned to accept smaller spaces. It is natural for you now to bump into doors, walls, your shoes always scuffed on one toe from taking too small a stride. You have back problems from stooping so as to appear smaller. You are familiar with the script as though it is some terrible show in syndication. You follow the prompt like your mother and hers. You accept your invitation to apologize. You excuse yourself for this shame.

"Excuse me," you said earlier today, when a man entered the doorway you were already standing inside, wrinkling his face in frustration as though you had suddenly appeared to deter him. You skittered away, seething, even now, later at night, as you move about the kitchen making dinner with your husband, who bumps you on his way to the refrigerator and doesn't notice.

Extra Lives

I am searching for hearts. For mushrooms. For gold. I am hoping to stockpile enough energy that I might survive the inevitable damage, might be able to keep playing the game.

I'm not sure it's worth it though. The game is an infinite series of rounds and complex puzzles to see how far I can advance at work while still putting dinner on the table, how I can age gracefully while doing so much laundry. I'm always flickering, a shadow of myself about to vanish, desperate for an extra life to keep me going a bit longer. I'm always missing the hidden tunnel, the secret door, the cheat codes.

My husband is a gamer who moves seamlessly from his work as a computer programmer during the day to his recreation at night while I sputter from my transition from the professional to the personal. He plays games where he is expected to complete daily tasks—fetching, talking, killing—in order to be permitted to keep playing. This sounds like marriage, I tell him, thinking of the dishes, the dusting, the many domestic tasks lining up like stats in a heads-up display. He plays games where he rolls many-sided dice and imagines worlds where anything is possible—dungeons and dragons and endless free ale at an ogre's pub. I play the game where I try not to bite the heads off male coworkers who call me sweetheart, where I listen to women crying in bathroom stalls beside me, where I try to dodge the many slithering arms of male strangers, where I try to defeat the final boss at the voting booth.

A lifetime raised on video games has not prepared me for this. Even as a girl, I found the games unfulfilling. None of the characters were aspirational. There was no one I wanted to play. Zelda featured a princess, but you could only save her. James Bond was nothing but British bullets. Most of the time I played Tetris because I was practiced in the art of living like a puzzle, of figuring out how to maneuver myself to fit the expectations of others. Early on, I learned to work hard to keep things from piling up, to keep time from running out.

For a while, I liked Mario Kart, the way you could drive off the road, veer crooked from the path and cut through fields and water, the way the roads opened up like a rainbow, curving and swerving. I liked to start revving my engine with everyone else and then take off in a different direction, refusing to turn back no matter how many warning signs appeared on-screen. I didn't mind straying from the track even if it meant losing, but eventually the adults and other players started saying I couldn't drive and wasn't that just like a girl, and why didn't I want to play as Princess Peach, even though Toad was my favorite, a fungus free of gender.

The game I played most often was Aladdin. I was envious of his genie wishes, the way he could so easily access magic to fly among the stars. Extra lives were simply a matter of gathering loaves of bread, which littered the streets, hunger no challenge for a clever man. Beautiful Jasmine rarely appeared, though she was desirable and powerful, everyone's favorite. I tried to forget that only her future husband would be able to rule the kingdom, that no one cared what she wanted, that the entire story centered on deceiving her. Instead, I gathered bread and lives, flew my carpet through caves filled with glittering gold as I tried to escape the rising lava. In between childhood chores like helping my mother with the dishes or the cooking or the laundry, I played until I learned the trick to escape. But sometimes, I crashed into the cave walls and let the lava drown me, so tired of running I simply let my lives run out.

These days I rarely have time for games. Still, I find time to play the one where I call a friend and leave her an exhausted voicemail about how busy I am and then wait for her to call me back, which she does, but then I am unavailable, and she leaves an exhausted voicemail about how busy she is, and then I call and talk to her machine again. I play the one where tasks at work or home pile up like Tetris blocks all around and I wait for male colleagues or family members to assist but they are busy talking at the water cooler or watching football. I play the one where each night I take stock of my flickering heart and wonder if I really want to wake to play again the next day.

Evenings and weekends I am too exhausted to do much of anything. When I manage to talk to my girlfriends, they say the same between the baby's cries and baking pies. I picture us, losing lives, shrinking to half our size like video game figures, each of us waiting to discover the magic item that will restore us, allow us to grow back to our rightful strength. I wonder where our husbands get the energy to gather online each weekend to pretend to be soldiers or elves, to spend entire afternoons focused on virtual reality when their webcams reveal their wives shuffling back and forth behind them, tending to the children, tidying the house, staring dead-eyed into space. In between rounds, the men talk about their other games—brewing beer or playing golf, running marathons and learning to fly real planes because virtual simulators just weren't enough.

When I am angry, I ask my husband how he can play for so long with the daily challenges of our lives around us, though I am lucky and he does far more than most. I ask him how he can always win the game in order to keep going. He tells me that there are infinite lives in the games they play. There is always a way for his teammates to resurrect him, to bring him back to life. And they can always use coins to simply purchase more lives.

It reminds me of the time early in my childhood when I first began to play video games. The adults set me up with a controller to play against my toddler sister in front of the screen. Rapt, entranced, I tried and died, time and again, desperate to succeed in an imaginary world. Why couldn't I win, I wondered, growing frustrated and fitful. How could even a child beat me at the game?

"Calm down," the adults said. "Be a big girl."

A family member told me, a beer clutched in his hand, they had they rigged the game against me. I was playing against the computer, not my sister, who at some point had crawled off without me noticing, so intent I had been on proving myself. How foolish I was to believe I could ever win against the system. How the others had laughed and laughed at my inevitable failure.

Now I feel foolish for thinking things would ever be different. Most women I know have either quit their jobs to stay home with the kids and manage the demands of their households, or they flicker like dying characters in a video game, hovering like ghosts between their personal and professional lives, feeling guilty for failing at both. How they would love to simply insert more coins into an arcade game or digitally transfer money to an online platform to buy more time, more resources, more lives.

How they would love to simply begin again.

Men Teach Me How to Play Dungeons & Dragons

The first rule is to listen.

This is a game of imagination, so players don't simply move plastic tokens. Instead, they create unique characters with personalities and rich histories. The man explaining this to me on New Year's Eve, for instance, has decided to be an academic Wizard. His engineering degree means he is very smart, words carefully selected from the thesaurus and therefore a little clunky in his mouth, like he is wearing a dental guard. I'm the one with the PhD, a professor—of storytelling, actually—but in this world, the Wizard speaks to me verrry slowwwly. He interrupts to clarify. He has a mighty staff.

The Wizard informs me about the character I've imagined. Apparently, I am to be a druid healer—I exist to take care of others, fix those who are damaged fighting. Like Wizards.

"Are the creatures winged? Do they have blue scales and sing opera?" I ask. "Why don't I have a mortar and pestle to grind healing herbs into a poultice?"

"That's not how we play," says the Wizard. He repeats himself in case I don't understand. I want to ask what color his robes are, if he wrote his dissertation on palynology. I want to know if he studied spores from rare mushrooms like the ones that grow at the foot of the mountains near my village, glinting ocher-furred in the morning light as I pick them with my spindly purple fingers, hanging them to dry while the Vlla-Vlla beast chortles beside me.

The second rule is to follow directions.

I choose my name from a pre-selected list the Wizard provides. We begin the quest, two men and their female partners counting down the end of year, though we must all be men in this game. The character I imagine is neither male nor female, but gender, like names, must be selected.

Our band of travelers moves through the map in a straight line. I hear a stream and want to detour.

"That's not the right direction," the Wizard says.

We come across two paths diverged but cannot explore the woods I imagine salmon-colored and scented of marshmallow. The other woman playing is tasked with choosing the path.

"Are you sure you want to do that?" the Wizard asks in the tone he probably uses while doing their taxes.

We walk the Wizard's way.

Suddenly, we are surrounded by wolves. It is my turn.

"You want to attack," wises the Wizard, holding the dice out to me like jewels or a child's treat.

I want to cast a spell to talk to the animals, feed them some squirrel meat, rub soothing salve on their hurt paws.

"They're wolves," says the Wizard. "Just kill them."

We do. Rain beads off their pelts as we leave, and I want to cast a spell to see the future, watch pink flowers become their eyes, vine tendrils around their bright bones. As we travel away, the Wizard and his staff at the lead, a melancholy wail follows us. I want to cast a resurrection spell.

"Watch your dice, woman!" the Wizard cries when I toss them in a way that takes up too much space.

I'm confused, seeing as my character is a man. I hold myself quiet, still. This is what a druid healer does, after all, for it is better to hear the beat of bird wings or the sound of a snail, the glisten it leaves behind as an antidote to loneliness.

I hurt from the effort of holding motionless.

"I'll do the talking," he says when we get to the imaginary town. He asks lots of questions, repeating the answers back to the rest of us even though we are also in the goblin pub. I did not want to go through the town—a nearby cave was calling.

"Go to the cave," say the goblins.

"We must go to the cave," the Wizard proclaims.

There is a skirmish with blood bears on the way to the cave, and the Wizard is hurt. I almost feel for him there on the forest floor, his bloodied robes billowing.

"You must heal me," he commands before I begin my turn. Maybe his injury is the reason he's stopped handing over the dice, flinging them across the table at me instead, or using his hand to scatter the tower I make with the dice each time I conclude my turn.

"I built you to heal me," he insists. Even though I am a man, I feel the rib I sprung from, a twisted root in my side.

"What are you waiting for?" cries the Wizard as the clock lurches toward a new year where everything will be the same, people desperate to craft themselves different, circle from the predetermined path.

I grip the dice in my hands. I put them down.

"I'm going to rest," I decide.

"You can't," disapproves the Wizard, much smaller now that he is writhing on the ground. He crushes ocher-furred mushrooms beneath his protest. I gather them to make a stew.

"I rest," I repeat, studying the map. I am looking for places to deviate from the path. I am tired of walking in a straight line. I would like, instead, to explore. To build my character. This rushed climb to climax is tiresome. I spin instead, holding my hands out to summon velvet-flavored leaves.

I rest again on my next turn—perhaps I am a woman after all, deserving of rest the way I am deserving of extra instructions. The Wizard takes off his celebratory cardboard top hat and sighs, crossing his arms.

The Wizard is near death, pale and weak. He doesn't have the energy to summon fancy words, though plenty for condemnation. He will not look at me.

I collect flowers, befriend a furious blood bear, and trick a dragon into revealing its secrets and treasure without injury, despite the Wizard's protests that, "This is not how you play."

At last I announce, "I heal you." And because he has not looked at me since I began moving in circles, I add, "You're welcome."

All game, the Wizard has kept the gold for himself. He needs the armor, he insists, because he is the most important warrior. I motion to the dragon treasure I've captured.

"Buy yourself something nice," I offer.

The New Year's ball drops. Auld Lang Syne. A toast, though he will not bring his glass, like his eyes, to meet mine.

Strength newly summoned, he purchases a larger rod to lead the way.

Acknowledgments

Grateful acknowledgment to the editors of the journals where the following pieces first appeared, sometimes in slightly altered form.

DIAGRAM: "Stomp"
Lost Balloon: "Pocketed"
Under the Sun: "Giving Up"
Monkeybicycle: "Light as a Feather, Stiff as a Board"
Hobart: "Hug Your Mad"
Sweet: "Skip It"
Fractured: "Connect the Dots Love"
Pidgeonholes: "Constellate"
Brevity: "Mystery House"
CRAFT: "Dash"
Split Lip Magazine: "Men Teach Me How to Play Dungeons & Dragons"

To the many girls and women who shared their lives with me. You made me believe our stories were of value and that I might be a storyteller.

To the women in my family who helped me grow: Karen Montgomery, Julie Montgomery, Natalie Montgomery, Susan Wilson, and Sherri Gray.

To the kind of friends who become family: Annie Bierman, Daniel Froid, and Mitch Hobza.

To Allison Blevins, Kristiane Weeks-Rogers, and the Harbor Editions team for believing in this small book and helping deliver it into the wide world.

And to my partner, Braydn Reynolds, who has never made me feel small and who has helped me to build a big, beautiful life.

Sarah Fawn Montgomery is the author of *Quite Mad: An American Pharma Memoir* and *Halfway from Home*. She is also the author of *Nerve: Unlearning Workshop Ableism to Develop Your Disabled Writing Practice* and three poetry chapbooks. She is an Associate Professor at Bridgewater State University.

About Small Harbor Publishing

Small Harbor Publishing is a 501c3 nonprofit organization. Our goal is to publish unique and diverse voices. We are a feminist press, and we are committed to diversity and inclusion. We strive to bring new voices to a devoted and expanding readership.

Small Harbor Publishing began in 2018 with the first issue of *Harbor Review*. The magazine is an online space where poetry and art converse. *Harbor Review* quickly grew and now publishes reviews and runs multiple micro chapbook competitions, including the Washburn Prize and the Editor's Prize.

In July 2020, Small Harbor Publishing was officially incorporated and began Harbor Editions. Harbor Editions accepts submissions through a chapbook open reading period, a hybrid chapbook open reading period, the Marginalia Series, and the Laureate Prize.

In 2023, Harbor Anthologies began with a mission to promote texts that explore social justice issues and highlight marginalized writers.

If you would like to support Small Harbor Publishing, visit our "About" page at: smallharborpublishing.com/about.

www.ingramcontent.com/pod-product-compliance
Lightning Source LLC
Chambersburg PA
CBHW020213090426
42734CB00008B/1052